Rolf Heimann's
Head Spinners

1 •

easy

2 ••

not so easy

3 •••

a bit hard

4 ••••

very hard

Southwood Books Limited
3-5 Islington High Street
London N1 9LQ

First published in Australia by Roland Harvey Books, 1999

This edition published in the UK under licence from
Penguin Books Australia Ltd by Southwood Books Limited, 2002

ISBN 1 903207 80 0

Copyright ©Rolf Heimann 1999

Film by Eray Scan, Singapore

A CIP catalogue record for this book is available from the British
Library.

Printed by Everbest, China

SOUTHWOOD
B O O K S

The path through a maze is often like the path through life, as the little mazes below show. Sometimes we choose the long way when a more direct path would have been best. Sometimes we have to return to the start to make it to the goal. Sometimes there are many different paths which will get us there. Difficult-looking problems may turn out to be the easiest while simple-looking ones may be no way out at all! This also teaches us a valuable lesson, namely you don't always get your money back if things don't work out!

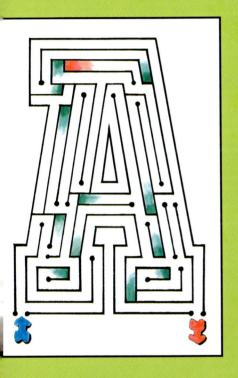
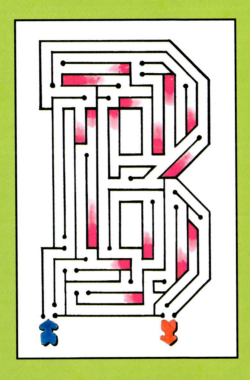
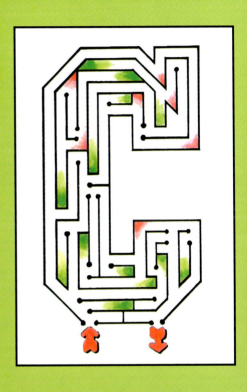
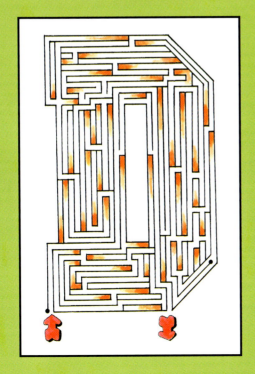
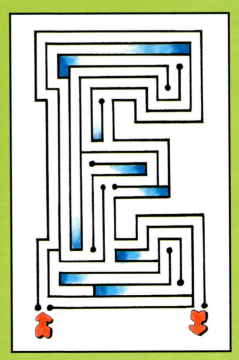

Mazeville

Five characters are on their way home to Mazeville.

Can you guess where they live and help them find their way? (Solution: page 30)

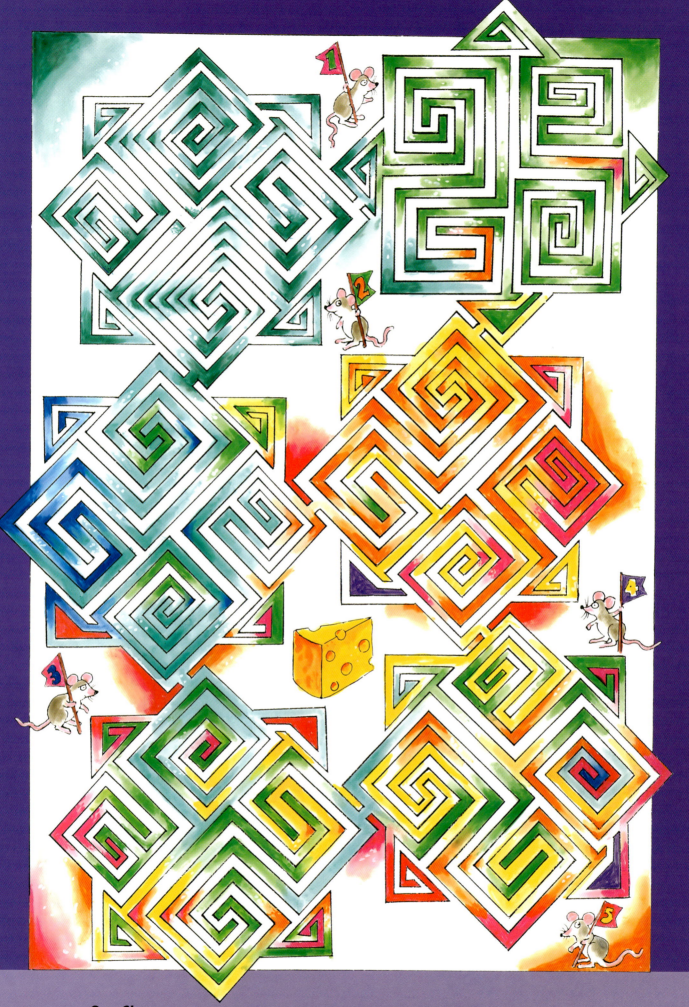

Say Cheese

Five mice are trying to get to the cheese. Will they be able to?

(Solution: page 30)

That's how the pyramid looks from above:

(Solution: page 30)

Pyramid

Imagine the pyramid being unfolded,
the base being the black triangle.
There are several ways of 'unfolding' it,
but the arrow must always point to the top
and the colours must stay in the same order.
Some of the examples are wrong. Which ones?

(Solution: page 30)

Make the Connection

Find the objects which belong to the people
and things below and fill in the corresponding
letters. But look carefully, the panels overlap!

(Solution: page 30)

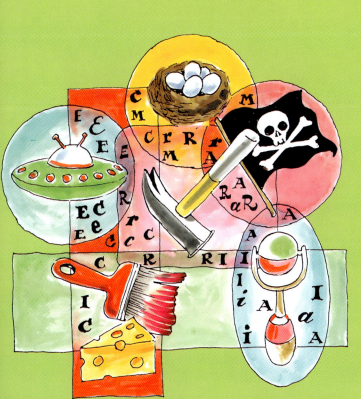

Watercastle

Tom, Lila and Ben arrived in the yellow boat and want to leave in the blue one.
Help them find their way across the island fortress.

9

⋯3

Doubleword

If you find it hard to make up a word, be inspired by the words below:

EARNEST, ANTHEM, SKILLED, BLOODSHED, COMBAT, NUTSHELL, MONKEY, HANDICAP, HATRED, COWARDICE, STARCH, CHOPSTICKS, MINESWEEPER.

Barbed Wire Maze

Don't get stuck as you go from top to bottom.

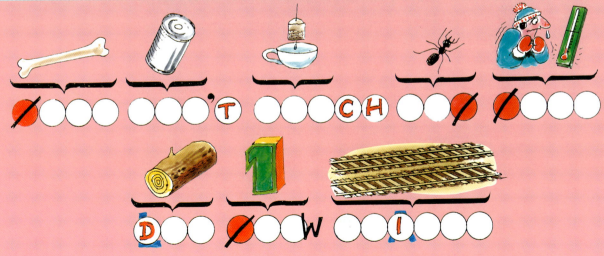

Rebus

Here's a hint: if you're a puppy, you might learn something! (Solution: page 30)

Snakessssss!

Snakekeeper Enrico has to take Annabelle the Patagonian Asp for her yearly check-up.

So that he could find her, he brought along Annabelle's picture. But spotting her is not so easy, is it?

Before you count them, guess how many snakes there are in this picture: 27? 41? 53? (Solution: page 30)

Tentacle Spectacle

Rover the yellow sardine has lost his way.

Can he find his way back to his school through the maze of tentacles?

(Solution: page 30)

Snap!

Major McKlink has to make an emergency landing on the planet of Snappio II, which is inhabited by the multicoloured Snapponoids. Luckily they are not as dangerous as they look; the only poisonous ones are the two-coloured ones. Those with more than two colours are quite harmless. Is there a two-coloured Snapponoid among them?

(Solution: page 30)

Double-Maze
There are two ways to get through this maze; either through the hedges or along the orange path.

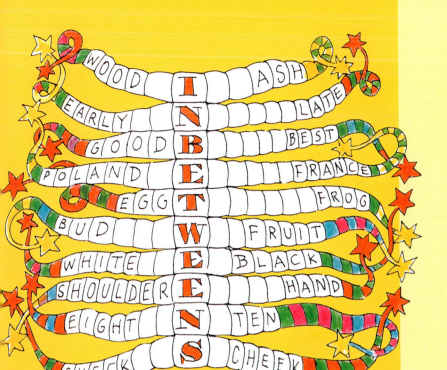

WOOD ... ASH
EARLY ... LATE
GOOD ... BEST
POLAND ... FRANCE
EGG ... FROG
BUD ... FRUIT
WHITE ... BLACK
SHOULDER ... HAND
EIGHT ... TEN
CHEEK ... CHEEK

IN BETWEENS

 2

In-Bit-Tweens

There's always something in between. Fill in the right words. For instance, between wood and ash is fire!

(Solution: page 30)

Nothing shall come between us!

It's the same thing.

And again!

Relativity

Everything is relative! The first answer is given to show you what you are expected to do. Don't just fill in the right words, draw the right thing. (Solution: page 30)

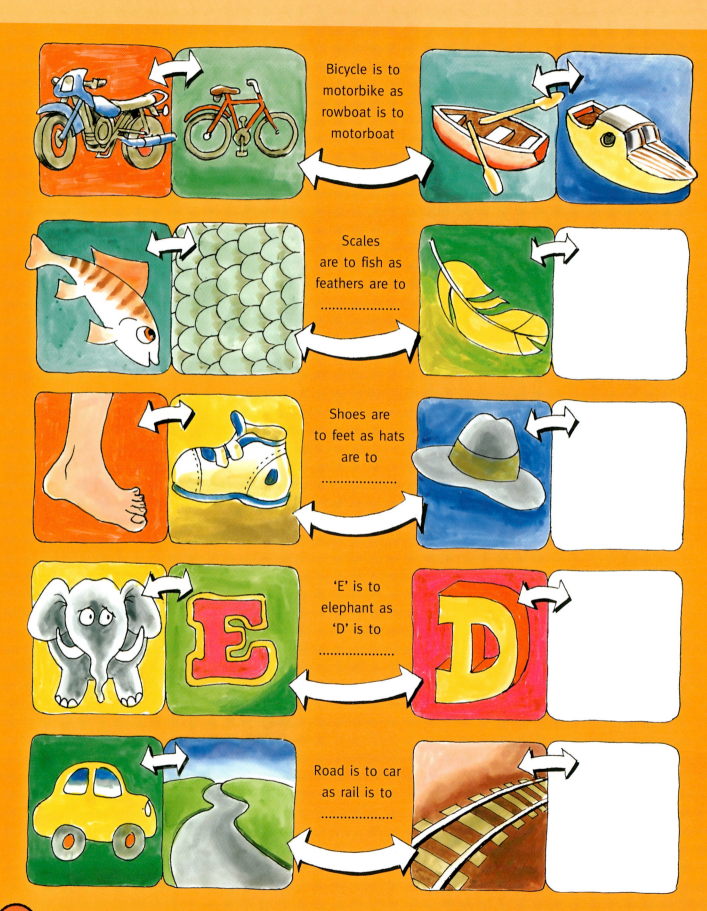

Bicycle is to motorbike as rowboat is to motorboat

Scales are to fish as feathers are to ....

Shoes are to feet as hats are to ....

'E' is to elephant as 'D' is to ....

Road is to car as rail is to ....

Now try making up some on your own! There are some ideas on page 30.

Dragon Maze

All seven snails will try to make their way through the maze to the leaves on the other side.
Not all of them can! Which ones will make it and which ones will not? (Solution: page 30)

Be a Detective!

Fingerprints are a great means of identification.

One of the ten prints is the same as the one under the magnifying glass.

Which one? Be careful, somebody's life might depend on it!

(Solution: page 31)

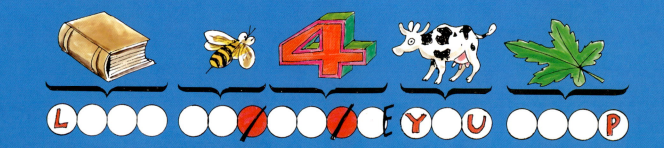

22

●●●●●▶4

Rhyme and Reason

Rat rhymes with hat! But that's all the advice you'll get for this puzzle.
The other rhymes you'll have to find yourself.
If you fill in the right letters, you'll get the name of a famous city.

(Solution: page 31)

●●●●▶3

Space Captain

Test your memory – or that of your friends! You are the captain of the space patrol No. 55 and you are exactly halfway to the galaxy of Nymropia when suddenly another ship appears. A strange green creature from the local Star Watch gets out. According to Intergalactic law you must answer him truthfully. Which question? Before you turn to the next page to read the question, study the picture and this text carefully. If you do, you'll be able to answer.

23

From previous page:
The green creature's question to patrol boat No. 55 is: 'What is the name of your captain?'

24

What's a Gazebo?
The shingles for the gazebo's roof have arrived. But how to get there?

What's the opposite of the big-eared spotted confuscus?

The earless spotless smarticus— which could be me!

The Big-Eared Spotted Confuscus
Transfer the lines onto the right squares below.
The position of the coloured border should be enough of a guide.

(Solution: page 31)

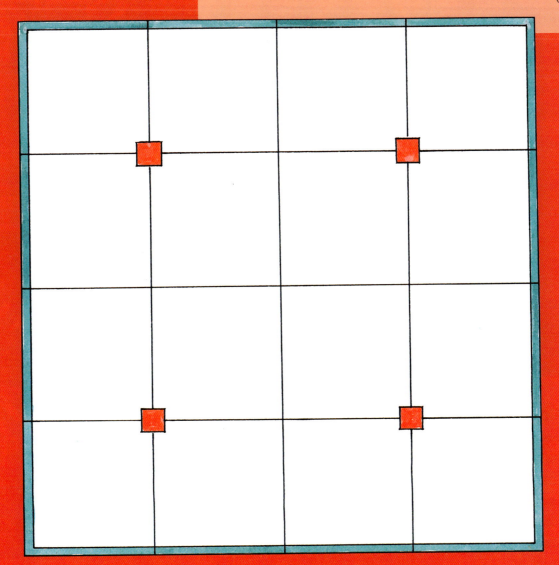

25

PICNIC ON
HANGING ROC

DATE	SCENE	TAKE
4/6	28	4

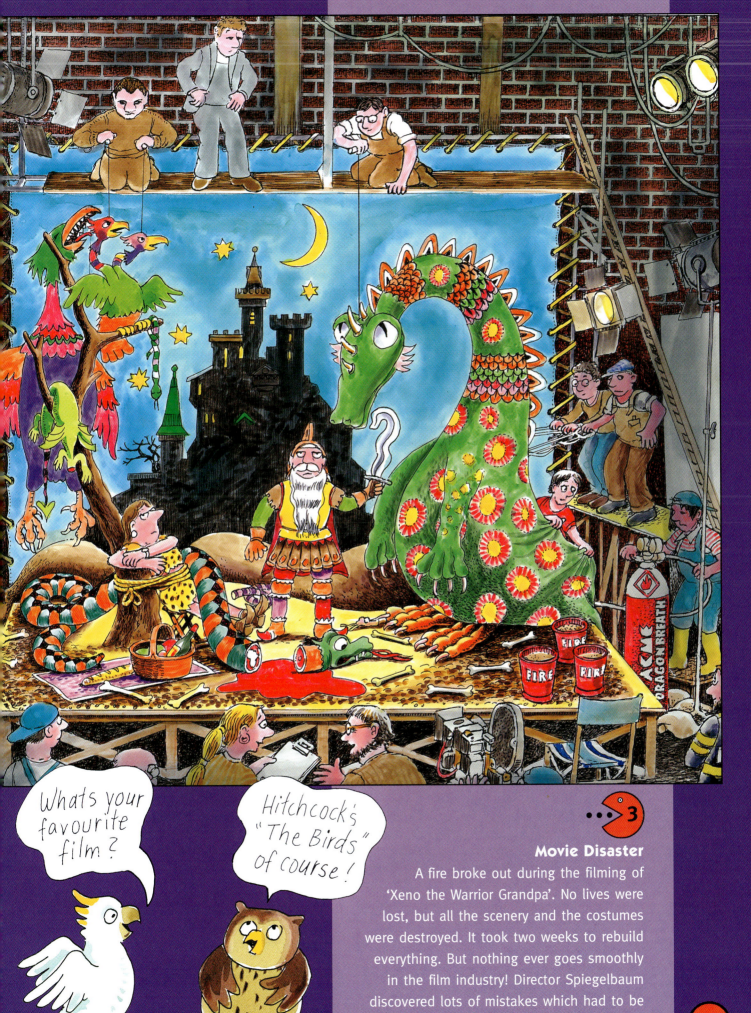

•••>3

Movie Disaster

A fire broke out during the filming of 'Xeno the Warrior Grandpa'. No lives were lost, but all the scenery and the costumes were destroyed. It took two weeks to rebuild everything. But nothing ever goes smoothly in the film industry! Director Spiegelbaum discovered lots of mistakes which had to be rectified before filming could continue. What were they? (Solution: page 31)

29

Solutions

page 4-5, Mazeville

page 6, Say Cheese

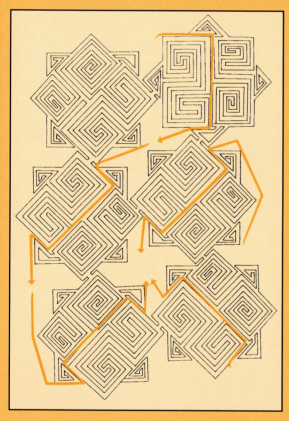

page 7, Pyramid

Pyramid A, G and I are the odd ones out.

page 7, Make the Connection

AMERICA

page 11, Rebus

'One can't teach an old dog new tricks.'

page 12, Snakesssss!

Annabelle is the snake right above Enrico's head.
There are 53 snakes in the picture.

page 13, Tentacle Spectacle

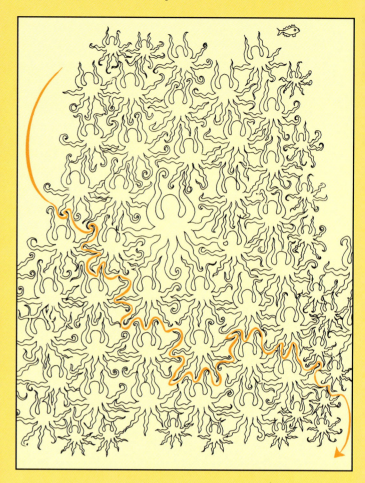

page 14-15, Snap!

The dangerous two-coloured snapponoid is the
yellow/red one right below Major McKlink.

page 17, In-Bit-Tweens

The In-Bit-Tweens are:

FIRE, PUNCTUAL, BETTER, GERMANY,

TADPOLE, FLOWER, GREY, ELBOW, NINE, NOSE.

It's the same thing: dragonfly

And again: carpet

page 18-19, Relativity

Scales are to fish as feathers are to bird.

Shoes are to feet as hats are to head.

'E' is to elephant as 'D' is to dog.

Road is to car as rail is to train.

New Zealand is to kiwi as Africa is to giraffe.

Window is to house as eye is to body.

'A' is to 'B' as '1' is to '2'.

Stripes are to zebra as spots are to tiger.

Ideas for your own:

Puppy is to dog as kitten is to cat.

Nest is to bird as cave is to bear.

Green is to grass as blue is to sky.

page 20-21, Dragon Maze

Snails 6 and 7 can make it to leaf C.

page 22, Be a Detective!

Fingerprint 'D' is the same as the one under the magnifying glass.

page 23, Rhyme and Reason

Hat rhymes with rat: C

Nail rhymes with tail: H

Ants rhymes with pants: I

Bat rhymes with rat: C

Bag rhymes with flag: A

Match rhymes with patch: G

Snake rhymes with cake: O

THE ANSWER IS CHICAGO

page 23, Space Captain

What, you don't know your own name? The copy suggests that you are the captain! (Your friend will surely fall for that one too.)

page 25, The Big-Eared Spotted Confuscus

page 26-27, Upside-Down Pyramid

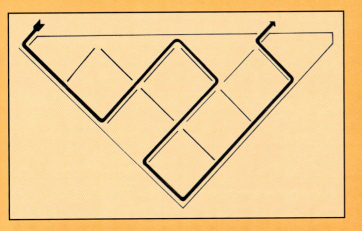

Here are the things which the people are doing the wrong way around:

- arrow the wrong way on bow
- sitting back to front on chairs
- hats on feet and socks on head
- old man with rattle and baby with walking cane
- dog leads man on leash
- gloves on feet and boots on hand
- keyhole beside door
- entering through window
- baby in coffin and dead man in cradle
- horse behind cart
- 'dimaryp' is 'pyramid' backwards
- The panel that says 'beware of fools who worship mice' is right at the bottom.

page 28-29, Movie Disaster:

ZZZZZZZ!
Can you show the snails the way?